GW00367667

First published in Great Britain by Hamlyn
This edition published in 1996 by Chancellor Press
an imprint of Reed Consumer Books Limited,
Michelin House, 81 Fulham Road, London SW3 6RB

ISBN 1 85153 003 7

A CIP catalogue record for this book
is available from the British Library

ACKNOWLEDGEMENTS

Designed and produced by: The Bridgewater Book Company
Series Editors: Veronica Sperling and Christine McFadden
Art Director: Peter Bridgewater
Designer: Terry Jeavons
Photography: Trevor Wood
Food preparation and styling: Jonathan Higgins
Cookery contributor: Christine France

Produced by Mandarin Offset
Printed and bound in Singapore

NOTES

❦ Standard level spoon measurements are used in all recipes.
❦ Both imperial and metric measurements have been given in all recipes. Use one set of measurements only and not a mixture of both.
❦ Eggs should be size 3 unless otherwise stated.
❦ Milk should be full fat unless otherwise stated.
❦ Fresh herbs should be used unless otherwise stated. If unavailable use dried herbs as an alternative but halve the quantites stated.
❦ Ovens should be preheated to the specified temperature - if using a fan assisted oven, follow manufacturer's instructions for adjusting the time and the temperature.
❦ All microwave information is based on a 650 watt oven. Follow manufacturer's instructions for an oven with a different wattage.

Contents

Introduction

THE baked jacket potato is a classic standby for all kinds of meal occasions. Transformed with a wide array of fillings or toppings it can be served as a satisfying snack, an accompaniment to a hot or cold main course, or a complete meal on its own.

All the recipes in this book are for hot, freshly-baked potatoes, unless otherwise stated.

The Perfect Baked Potato

The best potatoes to choose for baking are floury varieties, which include Cara, Desiree, Golden Wonder, King Edward, Maris Piper, Pentland Crown, Pentland Dell, Pentland Squire, Romano, and Wilja.

Choose large, even-sized potatoes with unblemished skins, weighing about 200 g/7 oz each.

Basic Recipe

SERVES 4

4 large baking potatoes
100 g/4 oz butter
salt and freshly ground black pepper

SCRUB the potatoes and dry well. Carefully cut away any damaged parts and prick the skins with a fork to allow steam to escape.

❦ Place in a preheated oven at 220°C/425°F/gas mark 7 for 1–1½ hours, directly on the shelf or in a roasting tin. The cooking time will depend on the size of potatoes.

❦ To check if the potatoes are cooked, squeeze gently – they should feel soft to the touch.

❦ Cut a cross in the top of each potato and squeeze the sides gently to open up. Top with butter and sprinkle with salt and pepper, or serve with your chosen filling.

TIPS: if you prefer a soft skin, wrap the potatoes in kitchen foil before baking.
For extra crusty, crisp skins, rub the skins with oil and sprinkle with salt before baking.

Alternative Methods For Jacket Potatoes

POTATO BAKER: these have metal prongs to spear through the potatoes, which help conduct the heat more quickly and reduce the cooking time. You can improvise by simply pushing a metal skewer through each potato before baking.

MICROWAVE: prick the potatoes as usual and wrap each in absorbent kitchen paper. Cook on High (100%) power for about 5–6 minutes for one potato, 10–12 minutes for two, or 18–20 minutes for four.

BONFIRE OR BARBECUE BAKING: cooking times can be unreliable, so the easiest way to do this is to bake them first in the oven for about 30 minutes as in the basic recipe, then wrap in foil and place them in the hot ashes around the edges of the fire to finish cooking.

WEDGES: cut each potato into 8 wedges. To microwave, place in a microwave dish with 1 tbsp water, cover with cling film and cook on High (100%) power for 6 minutes, or until tender. To bake, place in an ovenproof dish and brush with oil, then bake for about 30 minutes at 220°C/425°F/gas mark 7.

NEW POTATOES: cut in half and place on a large piece of buttered foil. Sprinkle with salt and pepper, seal the foil and place on a baking sheet in a preheated oven at 180°C/350°F/gas mark 4 for about 1 hour.

Simple Butters for Baked Potatoes

The easiest way to top a jacket potato is with a flavoured butter. You will need about 25g/1 oz per potato.
Beat 100 g/4 oz butter until soft, then stir in any of the following mixtures:

GARLIC BUTTER
1 garlic clove, crushed
1 small onion, finely chopped
salt and freshly ground black pepper
2 tbsp dry white wine
2 tbsp chopped fresh parsley

TOMATO & SESAME BUTTER
1 tbsp tomato purée
1 tbsp sesame seeds, toasted
salt and freshly ground black pepper

HERB BUTTER
1 tbsp snipped fresh chives
1 tbsp chopped fresh parsley
2 tsp lemon juice
salt and freshly ground black pepper

SPICY TABASCO BUTTER
1 tsp Tabasco sauce
1 tsp tomato purée
salt and cayenne pepper

GOLDEN CAPER BUTTER
2 tsp chopped capers
½ tsp ground turmeric
1 tbsp mayonnaise
1 tbsp dry white wine
salt and freshly ground black pepper

CLOCKWISE FROM THE FRONT: *Tomato and Sesame Butter, Garlic Butter, Herb Butter.*

Broccoli, Corn and Cheese

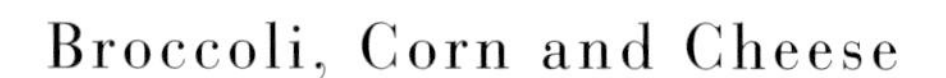

SERVES 4

150 g/5 oz broccoli
4 baked potatoes
15 g/½ oz butter
200 g/7 oz can sweetcorn, drained
salt and freshly ground black pepper
4 tbsp grated Edam cheese

Cut the broccoli into small florets and cook in boiling, lightly salted water until just tender. Drain well.

❦ Cut the potatoes in half and scoop out the flesh, leaving a thick shell. Chop the flesh, and add the butter, broccoli and sweetcorn.

❦ Season generously with salt and pepper and spoon back into the potatoes.

❦ Sprinkle with the cheese, and place under a preheated grill until just melted. Serve hot.

Mushrooms and Brie

SERVES 4

15 g/½ oz butter
1 small onion, finely chopped
1 garlic clove, crushed
200 g/7 oz button mushrooms, sliced
1 tbsp Worcestershire sauce
salt and freshly ground black pepper
150 g/5 oz brie
4 baked potatoes
2 tbsp snipped fresh chives

Melt the butter and fry the onion until soft. Add the garlic and mushrooms and stir over a low heat for 5 minutes or until the mushrooms are soft.

❦ Stir in the Worcestershire sauce and seasoning. Chop the brie and stir into the mixture. Heat gently until the cheese just begins to melt.

❦ Cut the potatoes in half and scoop out the flesh, leaving a thick shell. Mix the flesh into the mushrooms and season well with salt and pepper.

❦ Spoon back into the potatoes and serve hot, sprinkled with snipped chives.

Savoury Soufflé

SERVES 4

4 baked potatoes
50 g/2 oz butter
3 tbsp double or whipping cream
2 egg yolks
75 g/3 oz Cheddar cheese, grated
salt and freshly ground black pepper
2 egg whites, stiffly beaten

Cut each potato in half, and scoop out the flesh into a mixing bowl. Arrange all the potato shells in a baking dish.
❦ Add the butter, cream, egg yolks and 50 g/2 oz of the grated cheese to the potato flesh. Beat together well, and season to taste with salt and freshly ground black pepper.
❦ Fold in the beaten egg whites, and carefully spoon into the potato skins. Sprinkle with the remaining cheese, and bake in a preheated oven at 190°C/375°F/gas mark 5 for 15 minutes. Serve immediately.

Poached Egg Hollandaise

SERVES 4

2 egg yolks
100 g/4 oz unsalted butter, softened
1 tbsp lemon juice or
white wine vinegar
pinch of salt
4 eggs
2 large baked potatoes

Place the egg yolks and 15 g/½ oz of the butter in a small mixing bowl set over a pan of simmering water. Whisk together until creamy.
❦ Add the lemon juice or wine vinegar and salt, and continue whisking until the mixture has thickened slightly.
❦ Gradually whisk in the remaining butter, a little at a time, whisking until the sauce is very thick. Taste for seasoning and keep warm.
❦ Poach the eggs until the whites are set and the yolks still runny. Drain.
❦ Cut each potato in half. Scoop out a little of the flesh, to make a space for the egg. Place the eggs in the potatoes, pour over the hollandaise sauce and serve at once.

VARIATION: place a piece of finely sliced ham under each egg, and top with the hollandaise seasoned with 1–2 teaspoons made English mustard.

Spinach and Feta

SERVES 4

4 baked potatoes
1 tbsp sunflower oil
1 garlic clove, chopped
450 g/1 lb fresh young spinach leaves
100 g/4 oz feta cheese, diced
2 tbsp sunflower seeds
salt and freshly ground black pepper

HALVE the potatoes and scoop out the flesh, leaving a thick shell.

❦ Heat the oil and fry the garlic gently, without browning, for about 30 seconds.

❦ Add the spinach and stir-fry for 2–3 minutes, until wilted.

❦ Stir in the potato flesh, cheese and sunflower seeds, and heat thoroughly.

❦ Season well with salt and pepper, then spoon back into the shells and serve at once.

Spiced Aubergine and Lentils

SERVES 4

2 tbsp olive oil
½ tsp turmeric
½ tsp paprika
50 g/2 oz split red lentils
200 ml/7 fl oz stock
salt and freshly ground black pepper
1 small aubergine, sliced
2 large baked potatoes
4 tsp plain yogurt
paprika, to garnish

HEAT 1 teaspoon of the oil in a small pan and cook the spices, stirring, for about 30 seconds. Add the lentils and stock. Cover and simmer for about 15 minutes or until tender and most of the liquid is absorbed. Season to taste.

❦ Heat the remaining oil, and fry the aubergine slices over moderate heat for about 5 minutes, until tender and golden, turning once.

❦ Cut the potatoes in half, and arrange overlapping slices of aubergine over each half. Spoon over the lentils and top with a spoonful of yogurt.

❦ Sprinkle with paprika and serve hot.

Red Pepper and Garlic Dip with Potato Skins

SERVES 4

2 medium red peppers, halved and seeded
1 garlic clove
1 tbsp lemon juice
1 tbsp olive oil
3 tbsp fresh white breadcrumbs
salt and freshly ground black pepper
4 hot or cold baked potatoes

PLACE the peppers and garlic in a pan and add just enough water to cover. Bring to the boil, cover and simmer for 15 minutes or until tender. Drain well and cool.

❦ Place in a blender or food processor with the lemon juice and olive oil. Process until smooth.

❦ Stir in the breadcrumbs and season to taste.

❦ Cut the potatoes into quarters lengthways. Scoop out most of the flesh (use this for another recipe). Brush the skins with oil and place under a preheated grill for about 5 minutes, turning occasionally, until crisp and golden. Serve hot, with the dip.

Potato Skins with Soured Cream Dip

SERVES 4

150 ml/¼ pint soured cream
1 tsp snipped fresh chives
salt and freshly ground black pepper
4 baked potatoes
vegetable oil, for frying

TO MAKE the dip, place the soured cream in a mixing bowl, and stir in the chives. Season to taste. Cover and leave to chill in the refrigerator.

❦ Cool the baked potatoes for a few minutes, then cut each one into quarters lengthways.

❦ Using a teaspoon, scoop out most of the flesh, leaving just a thin layer next to the skin. (Use the potato flesh to top a pie.)

❦ Pour the oil into a small pan to a depth of 7.5 cm/3 inches. There is no need to use a large deep-frying pan.

❦ Heat the oil to 180–190°C/350–375°F, or until a cube of bread browns in 30 seconds.

❦ Fry 4–5 potato skins at a time for about 2 minutes until brown and crisp. Lift from the oil with a slotted spoon and drain on paper towels. Keep the skins hot in the oven while the remaining skins are cooked.

❦ Either sprinkle the skins lightly with salt or provide salt for guests to help themselves. Serve with the chilled dip, and a bowl of finely chopped tomatoes and spring onions, if liked.

Baked Potato Surprises

SERVES 4

4 baked potatoes
25 g/1 oz butter
4 eggs
salt and freshly ground black pepper
50 g/2 oz Cheddar cheese, grated

When the baked potatoes are cool enough to handle, cut a 'lid' out of the top of each – not quite cutting through on one side, so that the lid remains attached. Scoop out some of the flesh.

❦ Drop a knob of butter into each potato, followed by an egg, taking care not to break the yolk. Season with salt and pepper, sprinkle with the grated cheese and arrange the potatoes in an ovenproof dish. Bake in a preheated oven at 200°C/400°F/gas mark 6 for 15 minutes or until the eggs are set. Serve immediately.

Spicy Kidney Bean and Tomato

SERVES 4

1 tbsp oil
1 onion, chopped
1 green pepper, seeded and chopped
1 celery stick, chopped
400 g/14 oz can chopped tomatoes
400 g/14 oz can kidney beans
1–2 tsp chilli powder
salt and freshly ground black pepper
4 baked potatoes

Heat the oil in a saucepan and fry the onion, pepper and celery over medium heat until softened.

❦ Drain the canned tomatoes and reserve the juice. Stir the tomatoes into the mixture with the kidney beans, chilli powder, and salt and pepper to taste. Add a little of the tomato juice, then simmer, uncovered, for 30 minutes or until reduced to a fairly thick consistency.

❦ Cut a slit in each baked potato, pour over the filling and serve immediately.

Cottage Cheese, Apple and Peanut

SERVES 4

200 g/7 oz cottage cheese
1 crisp eating apple, cored and diced
salt and freshly ground black pepper
4 baked potatoes
50 g/2 oz salted peanuts or cashews

Mix together the cottage cheese and apple. Season to taste with salt and pepper.
❦ Cut a deep cross in each potato and press the sides to open out slightly.
❦ Spoon in the cheese and apple mixture, and scatter the nuts over. Serve immediately.

Cream Cheese and Chives

SERVES 4

100 g/4 oz cream cheese
1 small onion, finely chopped
1 tbsp snipped fresh chives
salt and freshly ground black pepper
4 baked potatoes
snipped fresh chives, to garnish

Place the cheese in a mixing bowl, and beat in the onion and chives. Season to taste with salt and pepper.
❦ Cut each potato in half, and scoop out the flesh into the mixing bowl. Mix well together, then pile the mixture back into the potato shells. Serve immediately, garnished with extra snipped chives.

VARIATION: cottage cheese or curd cheese can be substituted for the cream cheese.

Mushrooms and Garlic

SERVES 4

50 g/2 oz butter
2 garlic cloves, finely sliced
100 g/4 oz mushrooms, sliced
1–2 tbsp chopped fresh mixed herbs (e.g. parsley, chervil and thyme)
salt and freshly ground black pepper
4 baked potatoes

MELT the butter in a saucepan. Add the garlic and mushrooms. Cover and cook for about 5 minutes, stirring occasionally, until the mushrooms are just tender.
❦ Stir in the herbs, and season with salt and pepper to taste.
❦ Cut a deep cross in the top of each baked potato and squeeze gently to open. Spoon in the mushroom filling and serve immediately.

Ratatouille

SERVES 4

4-6 tbsp olive oil
1 medium aubergine, sliced
450 g/1 lb tomatoes, skinned and roughly chopped
1 green pepper, cored, seeded and sliced
450 g/1 lb courgettes, sliced
350 g/12 oz onions, sliced
1 large garlic clove, crushed
pinch of caster sugar
salt and freshly ground black pepper
1 bay leaf
4 baked potatoes
freshly grated Parmesan cheese, to serve

HEAT the oil in a large flameproof casserole. Mix the aubergine with the tomatoes, sliced pepper, courgettes, onion and garlic. Add them to the oil in batches, if necessary, and fry for about 8 minutes, turning occasionally.
❦ Stir in the sugar and plenty of salt and pepper. Add the bay leaf, cover and cook in a preheated oven at 160°C/325°F/gas mark 3 for 1½–2 hours or until the vegetables are soft.
❦ Cut the baked potatoes almost in half and open out. Spoon over the hot ratatouille and serve immediately with grated Parmesan cheese.

Gado-Gado

SERVES 4

4 baked potatoes
1 small onion, thinly sliced
1 tbsp oil
1 garlic clove, crushed
½ tsp chilli powder
1 small carrot, thinly sliced
1 small courgette, diced
3 tbsp smooth peanut butter
1 tbsp lemon juice
3 tbsp water
salt and freshly ground black pepper
chopped peanuts

CUT THE potatoes in half and scoop out the flesh, leaving a thick shell.

❦ Fry the onion in the oil until softened. Stir in the garlic and chilli powder.

❦ Add the carrot and courgette, and stir-fry for 2–3 minutes. Stir in the potato flesh, and cook for a further 2 minutes.

❦ Add the peanut butter, lemon juice, water, salt and pepper. Spoon the mixture into the potatoes, and sprinkle with chopped peanuts to serve.

Guacamole

SERVES 4

2 ripe avocados
1 tsp fresh red chilli, finely chopped or ½ tsp chilli powder
1–2 tbsp lemon or lime juice
2–3 tbsp olive oil
salt
1 small onion, finely chopped
1 garlic clove, crushed
2 tomatoes, skinned and chopped
4 baked potatoes
black olives, to garnish

PEEL and stone the avocados. Place the flesh in a mixing bowl, and mash with the chilli and lemon or lime juice, adding as much oil as can be absorbed. Season the mixture with salt and carefully stir in the onion, garlic and tomatoes.

❦ Cut a cross in the top of each baked potato, and squeeze gently to open them up. Pile in the filling, and garnish with black olives.

Blue Cheese, Celery and Almond Soufflés

SERVES 4

4 baked potatoes
1 celery stick, sliced
15 g/½ oz butter
75 g/3 oz dolcelatte or other blue cheese
2 eggs (size 2), separated
salt and freshly ground black pepper
2 tbsp flaked almonds

CUT the potatoes in half, scoop out the flesh into a mixing bowl and mash thoroughly.

❦ Fry the celery in the butter to soften slightly. Add to the mashed potato.

❦ Chop or crumble the cheese, and stir in with the egg yolks and seasoning.

❦ Whisk the egg whites until stiff and fold evenly into the potato mixture. Spoon back into the potato shells and sprinkle with almonds.

❦ Bake in an ovenproof dish in a preheated oven at 220°C/425°F/gas mark 7 for about 10 minutes, until golden brown and well risen.

Mascarpone, Basil and Sun-Dried Tomato

SERVES 4

6 tbsp mascarpone or cream cheese
50 g/2 oz sun-dried tomatoes, chopped
3 tbsp chopped fresh basil
4 baked potatoes
garlic salt and freshly ground black pepper
basil leaves, to garnish

MIX together the cheese, tomatoes and basil. Cut 3 deep slashes across each potato.

❦ Spoon the cheese mixture between each cut in the potatoes, and sprinkle with garlic salt and pepper.

❦ Garnish with basil, and serve immediately.

Aviyal (Mild Vegetable Curry)

SERVES 4

- 50 g/2 oz fresh or frozen shelled peas
- 2 carrots, chopped
- 3 tbsp vegetable oil
- 1 onion, finely chopped
- 1 green pepper, finely chopped
- 1 tsp ground turmeric
- 2 tsp ground coriander
- 2 tsp ground cumin
- 1 tsp mustard seeds
- ½ small cauliflower, broken into florets
- 2 tomatoes, skinned and chopped
- 100 g/4 oz okra, sliced
- salt and freshly ground black pepper
- 50–75 g/2–3 oz desiccated coconut
- 150 ml/¼ pint plain yogurt
- 4 baked potatoes

PARBOIL the peas and carrots in boiling salted water for about 3 minutes, so that they will be partially cooked when added to the sauce. Drain, reserving the cooking water.

❦ Heat the oil in a large heavy-based saucepan, and add the onion, pepper and all the spices. Fry over medium heat, stirring frequently, for 5 minutes.

❦ Add the remaining vegetables to the pan, season to taste, and pour in just enough reserved cooking water to moisten the mixture. Cook gently, stirring occasionally, and topping up the liquid if necessary, for about 10 minutes, or until the vegetables are tender but still crunchy. Be careful not to add too much water as the curry should be fairly dry at this stage.

❦ Sprinkle in coconut to taste, cook for a further 2 minutes, then add the yogurt. Remove the curry from the heat.

❦ Cut a cross in the top of each baked potato, and spoon in the filling. Serve with small side dishes of mango chutney and sliced cucumber in yogurt.

Mixed Bean, Thyme and Tomato

SERVES 4

- 1 small onion, thinly sliced
- 1 tbsp olive oil
- 225 g/8 oz can mixed bean salad
- 4 tbsp passata or tomato ketchup
- 1 tbsp chopped fresh thyme
- salt and freshly ground black pepper
- 4 baked potatoes
- thyme sprigs or oregano, to garnish

FRY THE onion in the oil until softened and lightly browned. Add the beans, passata and thyme. Cover and simmer for 3–4 minutes, until thoroughly heated. Season well.

❦ Cut the potatoes in half and scoop out the centres, leaving a thick shell. Chop the flesh roughly and stir into the beans.

❦ Bring the bean mixture to the boil, and spoon into the potatoes. Serve immediately, garnished with thyme or oregano.

Crunchy Cauliflower

SERVES 4

1 large cauliflower
175 g/6 oz Cheshire cheese, crumbled
150 ml/¼ pint soured cream
1 tbsp plain flour
25 g/1 oz butter
25–50 g/1–2 oz dried breadcrumbs
50 g/2 oz walnuts, coarsely chopped
1 tsp chopped fresh mixed herbs or ½ tsp dried
salt and freshly ground black pepper
4 baked potatoes

Break the cauliflower into florets, and cook in boiling salted water for 5 minutes, until just tender. Drain and arrange in a shallow ovenproof dish.
❦ Place the soured cream, flour and cheese in a mixing bowl, and stir to combine. Spoon the mixture over the cauliflower.
❦ Melt the butter in a small saucepan, stir in the breadcrumbs, walnuts, herbs, and salt and pepper to taste. Sprinkle the cauliflower with the mixture and bake in a preheated oven at 180°C/350°F/gas mark 4 for about 10 minutes or until golden and crisp.
❦ Cut each potato in half, spoon over the cauliflower filling, and serve immediately.

Beetroot and Red Onion

SERVES 4

4 baked potatoes
2 small cooked beetroot, diced
1 small red onion, halved
3 tbsp soured cream
1 tbsp chopped fresh dill
salt and freshly ground black pepper
sprigs of dill, to garnish

Halve the potatoes and scoop out the flesh, leaving a thick shell. Chop the flesh and mix with the beetroot.
❦ Finely chop half the onion and thinly slice the rest. Stir the chopped onion and soured cream into the beetroot mixture.
❦ Add the dill and seasoning, then spoon into the potato shells and top each with some sliced onion and a sprig of dill. Serve immediately.

Florentine Scramble Surprises

SERVES 4

4 baked potatoes
300 g/11 oz frozen chopped spinach, thawed
salt and freshly ground black pepper
3 eggs, beaten
2 tbsp milk
freshly grated nutmeg
15 g/½ oz butter

CUT the tops from each potato to form a lid and scoop out the flesh, leaving a thick shell. Mash the flesh.
❦ Place the spinach in a sieve and press out any excess moisture. Stir into the mashed potato. Season well with salt and pepper.
❦ Spoon back into the shells, leaving a hollow in the centre and piling the mixture up slightly above the sides.
❦ Beat the eggs and milk together, and season well. Cook over a moderate heat, stirring, until lightly set.
❦ Quickly spoon the scrambled eggs into the hollow of the potatoes. Sprinkle with nutmeg, dot with butter and replace the potato lids.
❦ Place in a preheated oven at 200°C/400°F/gas mark 6 for about 6–8 minutes, until hot (but don't overheat or the egg will set too firmly). Serve immediately.

Peperonata

SERVES 4

1 small onion, sliced
2 tsp olive oil
1 red pepper, seeded and sliced
1 yellow pepper, seeded and sliced
1 garlic clove, crushed
225 g/8 oz can tomatoes
salt and freshly ground black pepper
4 pitted black olives, quartered
4 baked potatoes

FRY the onion in the oil until soft. Stir in the peppers, garlic, tomatoes, and salt and pepper.
❦ Cover and simmer for 20–25 minutes, until the peppers are very soft and any liquid has evaporated. Stir in the olives, and season to taste.
❦ Cut a deep cross in each potato and press to open out. Spoon in the peperonata and serve hot.

Boston Baked Beans

SERVES 4

15 g/½ oz lard or butter
1 small onion, sliced
4 rashers streaky bacon, rinded and chopped
40 g/1½ oz muscovado sugar
1 tbsp black treacle
1 tsp made mustard
1 tsp salt
¼ tsp freshly ground black pepper
150 ml/¼ pint boiling water
425 g/15 oz can cannellini beans, drained
4 baked potatoes

MELT the lard or butter in a flameproof casserole dish, and fry the onion until soft.

❦ Add the bacon and fry, stirring frequently, until crisp. Mix in the sugar, treacle, mustard, salt, pepper and water. Bring to the boil, then simmer for 10 minutes. Stir in the beans.

❦ Cover and cook in a preheated oven at 180°C/350°F/gas mark 4 for 35 minutes.

❦ Cut a slit in the top of each baked potato, spoon in the filling and serve immediately.

Frankfurter and Mustard Bites

SERVES 4

15 g/1 oz butter or margarine
1 medium onion, sliced
4 frankfurters
4 baked potatoes
salt and freshly ground black pepper
4 tbsp English mustard

MELT the butter and fry the onion over medium heat until soft and golden brown.

❦ Add the frankfurters and cook, turning occasionally, for about 3 minutes until thoroughly heated through.

❦ Make a series of zig-zag cuts down the length of each potato and open out the 2 halves very carefully, leaving them joined at the base.

❦ Place a frankfurter in each and top with a spoonful of fried onion. Sprinkle with salt and pepper and pipe or spoon over the mustard. Serve immediately.

Chinese Porkers with Bean Sprouts

SERVES 4

225 g/8 oz lean pork shoulder or fillet
2 tsp sunflower oil
1 tsp chopped fresh ginger root
75 g/3 oz bean sprouts
1 tbsp light soy sauce
4 baked potatoes
salt and freshly ground black pepper
1 tbsp sesame seeds, toasted

Cut the pork into thin strips and stir-fry in the oil, stirring until golden brown.

❦ Add the ginger, bean sprouts and soy sauce and cook for a further 2 minutes.

❦ Cut the potatoes in half and scoop out the flesh. Chop and add to the pan. Season with salt and pepper and heat thoroughly.

❦ Spoon the mixture back into the potato shells, sprinkle with sesame seeds and serve hot.

BLTs (Bacon, Lettuce and Tomato)

SERVES 4

4 rashers streaky bacon
2 tomatoes
4 baked potatoes
4 crisp lettuce leaves, shredded
4 tbsp mayonnaise
salt and freshly ground black pepper

Cut the bacon rashers in half across the middle to make 2 shorter lengths. Grill or fry until crisp and browned.

❦ Cut the tomatoes into thin wedges.

❦ Make a deep cut down the length of each potato and open out, leaving them joined at the base.

❦ Fill the cut with shredded lettuce and top with the bacon and tomato wedges.

❦ Top each with a spoonful of mayonnaise and sprinkle with salt and pepper.

Bacon and Mushrooms

SERVES 4

225 g/8 oz streaky bacon, rinded and chopped
100 g/4 oz button mushrooms, sliced
4 baked potatoes
125 ml/4 fl oz soured cream
salt and freshly ground black pepper
2 tbsp snipped fresh chives
2 rashers streaky bacon, to garnish

FRY the chopped bacon in a frying pan over a moderate heat until crisp. Add the mushrooms, and cook for a further 5 minutes.

❦ Slice the tops off the potatoes, and scoop out the flesh into a bowl. Add the mushroom and bacon mixture, half the soured cream, and salt and pepper to taste. Fold in half the chives. Pile back high into the potato skins. Bake in a preheated oven at 190°C/375°F/gas mark 5 for 5–10 minutes.

❦ Meanwhile, pleat the bacon rashers onto a skewer. Place under a preheated hot grill and cook until golden.

❦ Remove the potatoes from the oven. Spoon over the remaining soured cream, top with the pleated bacon rashers and sprinkle with the remaining chives.

Cheesy Ham and Onion

SERVES 4

100 g/4 oz cooked ham
1 small onion
75 g/3 oz Cheddar cheese, grated
1 egg, beaten
pinch of salt and cayenne pepper
1 tsp made mustard
4 baked potatoes
40 g/1½ oz butter

PUT the ham and onion in a food processor and chop finely. Place in a mixing bowl and mix in 50 g/2 oz of the cheese, the beaten egg, salt, cayenne pepper and mustard.

❦ Cut the potatoes in half, and scoop out the flesh into the bowl. Add the butter and mix all the ingredients together.

❦ Pile the mixture back into the potato cases, and sprinkle with the remaining cheese.

❦ Wrap each potato in foil to enclose it completely, then bake for about 15 minutes in a preheated oven at 200°C/400°F/gas mark 6. Serve at once in the foil containers.

Peperoni Jackets

SERVES 4

15 g/½ oz butter or margarine
1 green pepper, seeded and chopped
4 baked potatoes
salt and freshly ground black pepper
50 g/2 oz sliced peperoni sausage or salami
3 small tomatoes, thinly sliced

Heat the butter and fry the pepper over a moderate heat, stirring, until tender but not browned.

❦ Halve the potatoes and scoop out the flesh. Chop roughly and stir into the pan. Season with salt and pepper.

❦ Pile the mixture back into the potato shells. Arrange overlapping slices of peperoni and tomato over each potato. Place on a baking sheet and cook under a hot grill for 3–4 minutes. Serve immediately.

Chilli con Carne

SERVES 4

1 tbsp oil
2 onions, sliced
1 garlic clove, crushed
450 g/1 lb minced beef
2 × 400 g/14 oz cans tomatoes
2 tsp chilli powder
½ tsp ground cumin
1 tbsp tomato purée
150 ml/¼ pint red wine
salt and freshly ground black pepper
1 bay leaf
425 g/15 oz can red kidney beans, drained
4 baked potatoes

Heat the oil in a heavy-based saucepan, and fry the onions and garlic over a low heat until softened. Add the beef and cook until browned, stirring to break up the lumps.

❦ Add the tomatoes with their juice. Bring to the boil, cover and simmer over a low heat for about 45 minutes, stirring occasionally. It may be necessary to add a little boiling water if the liquid evaporates.

❦ In a small bowl, blend the chilli powder with a little of the hot liquid from the beef. Stir this into the beef together with the cumin and tomato purée. Add the red wine, seasoning, bay leaf and drained beans. Cover and simmer for a further 1 hour, then discard the bay leaf.

❦ Cut a slit in the baked potatoes, and pile in the filling. Serve immediately, with a bowl of yogurt and a mixed green salad.

Spiced Moroccan Lamb

SERVES 4

225 g/8 oz lean minced lamb
1 small onion, sliced
1 tsp ground cumin
1 tsp ground coriander
50 g/2 oz no-soak dried apricots, chopped
2 tbsp ground almonds
1 tbsp tomato purée
4 baked potatoes
salt and freshly ground black pepper
4 tbsp Greek-style yogurt
chopped fresh coriander, to garnish

In a non-stick or heavy-based pan, fry the lamb and onion without fat, stirring until golden brown.
❦ Stir in the spices and cook for a further minute. Add the apricots, almonds and tomato purée.
❦ Cut a slice from the top of each potato and carefully scoop out the flesh. Chop roughly and add to the pan. Adjust the seasoning with salt and pepper.
❦ Spoon the mixture into the potatoes, top with the yogurt and garnish with coriander. Serve hot.

Creamy Ham, Leek and Cheese

SERVES 4

1 small leek
15 g/½ oz butter or margarine
75 g/3 oz smoked ham
4 baked potatoes
4 tbsp double cream
salt and freshly ground black pepper
50 g/2 oz Red Leicester cheese

Thinly slice the leek, and fry gently in the butter until soft but not browned. Remove from the heat. Dice the ham and add to the pan.
❦ Cut the potatoes in half and scoop out the flesh, leaving a thick shell. Add the flesh to the leek and ham.
❦ Stir in the cream and season with salt and pepper. Spoon back into the potato shells.
❦ Cut the cheese into thin strips and arrange over the potatoes. Place under a preheated hot grill until the cheese is just melted. Serve hot.

Minted Turkey and Yogurt

SERVES 4

225 g/8 oz turkey mince
1 small onion, thinly sliced
2 tbsp finely chopped fresh mint
4 tbsp plain yogurt
2 tsp lime juice
2 tsp clear honey
salt and freshly ground black pepper
4 baked potatoes
mint sprigs, to garnish

In a non-stick pan, fry the turkey mince without fat over medium heat until lightly coloured. Add the onion, and stir until lightly browned.

❦ Stir in the mint, yogurt, lime juice, honey, and season with salt and pepper.

❦ Bring to the boil, then reduce the heat, cover the pan and simmer for 10 minutes.

❦ Cut a deep cross in the potatoes and press the sides to open out. Spoon in the turkey mixture and serve hot, garnished with sprigs of mint.

Boxing Day Jackets

SERVES 4

4 baked potatoes
4 slices cooked turkey breast
8 tbsp herb stuffing
25 g/1 oz butter
salt and freshly ground black pepper
4 tbsp cranberry sauce
parsley sprigs, to garnish

Cut the potatoes almost in half lengthways, and open out. Place a turkey slice in each, with a spoonful of stuffing on either side. Dot with butter, and season generously with salt and pepper.

❦ Wrap each potato closely in foil, and place in a preheated oven at 200°C/400°F/gas mark 6 for about 15 minutes, until the turkey is thoroughly heated through.

❦ Unwrap the foil, and place a spoonful of cranberry sauce in each potato. Garnish with a parsley sprig, and serve hot.

Curried Chicken

SERVES 4

25 g/1 oz butter
1 small onion, finely chopped
1 tbsp curry powder
5 tbsp tomato juice
1 tbsp mango chutney
150 ml/¼ pint mayonnaise
225 g/8 oz cold cooked chicken, chopped
salt and freshly ground black pepper
4 baked potatoes

HEAT the butter in a saucepan, and fry the onion over low heat until softened. Stir in the curry powder and continue to cook, stirring, for 1 minute.

❦ Add the tomato juice and the mango chutney, and simmer over low heat for 2 minutes. Remove from the heat and allow to cool.

❦ Place the mayonnaise and chopped chicken in a mixing bowl, and stir in the cold curry mixture. Season to taste.

❦ Cut a cross in the top of each potato, squeeze gently to open them up, and spoon in the filling. Serve hot.

Chicken Tikka Masala

SERVES 4

4 tbsp plain yogurt
2 tsp garam masala
1 garlic clove, crushed
200 g/7 oz boneless skinless chicken, chopped
2 tsp sunflower oil
1 medium onion, chopped
1 medium tomato, diced
4 baked potatoes
1 tbsp chopped fresh coriander
salt and freshly ground black pepper

MIX together the yogurt, garam masala and garlic. Toss the chicken in this to coat evenly. Leave to marinate for about 1 hour.

❦ Heat the oil and fry the onion, stirring, until softened and lightly browned.

❦ Stir in the chicken and cook until lightly browned. Add the tomato, then cover and simmer for 5 minutes.

❦ Cut the potatoes in half and scoop out the flesh, leaving a thick shell. Chop the flesh roughly and add to the chicken with the coriander.

❦ Adjust the seasoning with salt and pepper. Spoon back into the potato shells and serve hot.

Barbecue Chicken and Mushroom

SERVES 4

1 tbsp sunflower oil
1 small onion, sliced
1 garlic clove, crushed
75 g/3 oz button mushrooms, quartered
2 tbsp tomato purée
1 tbsp light muscovado sugar
1 tbsp Worcestershire sauce
100 g/4 oz cooked chicken, diced
salt and freshly ground black pepper
4 baked potatoes

HEAT the oil and fry the onion for 3–4 minutes, until golden brown.
❦ Add the garlic and mushrooms and stir over a moderate heat until softened but not browned.
❦ Stir in the tomato purée, sugar, Worcestershire sauce and chicken. Season well with salt and pepper.
❦ Cut a deep cross in each potato and remove the flesh with a teaspoon, leaving a thick shell. Chop the potato flesh, stir into the chicken mixture and spoon back into the potatoes.
❦ Place in a preheated oven at 200°C/400°F/gas mark 6 for 10 minutes, then serve hot.

Chicken Satay with Coconut

SERVES 4

1 small onion, finely chopped
1 tbsp sunflower oil
1 tsp ground coriander
1 tsp chilli powder
100 g/4 oz crunchy peanut butter
1 tbsp tomato purée
1 tbsp clear honey
1 tbsp lime juice
200 ml/7 fl oz coconut milk
175 g/6 oz cooked chicken, diced
4 baked potatoes
shredded coconut and coriander leaves, to garnish

FRY the onion in the oil to soften. Stir in the spices and cook for 1 minute.
❦ Stir in the peanut butter, tomato purée, honey, lime juice and coconut milk. Bring to the boil, stirring.
❦ Add the chicken, cover and simmer gently for about 5 minutes, until thoroughly heated through.
❦ Cut the potatoes almost in half lengthways, and open out slightly. Spoon the chicken mixture into the potatoes, garnish with coconut and coriander and serve hot.

Turkey with Orange and Pecans

SERVES 4

4 baked potatoes
1 medium orange
200 g/7 oz cooked turkey, diced
50 g/2 oz pecan nuts or walnuts
100 g/4 oz cream cheese
salt and freshly ground black pepper

CUT the potatoes in half and scoop out the flesh, leaving a thick shell.

❦ Finely grate the zest from half the orange and remove a few strips of zest for garnish.

❦ Cut all the peel and white pith from the orange and remove the segments. Mix together the segments, potato flesh, turkey, pecan nuts and cream cheese.

❦ Pile the mixture back into the shells.

❦ Cover with foil and place in a preheated oven at 200°C/400°F/gas mark 6 for 10–15 minutes, or until thoroughly heated through.

❦ Sprinkle with the reserved orange zest, and serve hot.

Smoked Chicken and Kiwi

SERVES 4

200 g/7 oz boneless smoked chicken, diced
2 kiwi fruit, diced
3 tbsp mayonnaise
2 tbsp lemon juice
salt and freshly ground black pepper
4 hot or cold baked potatoes
2 tbsp flaked almonds, toasted

TOSS together the chicken and kiwi fruit. Mix together the mayonnaise and lemon juice, then stir in the chicken and kiwi fruit. Season well with salt and pepper.

❦ Cut a slice from the top of each potato and scoop out the flesh, leaving a thick shell. Chop and add to the chicken with the almonds.

❦ Spoon the mixture back into the potatoes and top with the lid. Serve hot or cold, for picnics or packed lunches.

Sherried Chicken Liver

SERVES 4

15 g/½ oz butter or margarine
225 g/8 oz chicken livers, chopped
3 spring onions, sliced
2 tbsp dry sherry
salt and freshly ground black pepper
4 baked potatoes
3 tbsp soured cream or Greek-style yogurt
spring onions, to garnish

MELT the butter in a frying pan, and fry the chicken livers, stirring, for 3–4 minutes.

❦ Add the onions and fry for a further minute, then add the sherry, and season with salt and pepper.

❦ Stir over the heat until the liquid is almost all evaporated. Stir in the soured cream or yogurt.

❦ Cut a deep cross in each potato and press the sides to open out. Spoon in the filling and garnish with spring onions. Serve immediately.

Cajun Chicken

SERVES 4

4 baked potatoes
1 tbsp corn oil
1 garlic clove, crushed
1 celery stick, chopped
150 g/5 oz boneless skinless chicken breast, chopped
1 tbsp tomato purée
1 tbsp lime juice
1 tsp hot chilli sauce (or ½ small green chilli, chopped)
celery salt and freshly ground black pepper
2 tbsp chopped fresh parsley, to garnish

CUT the potatoes in half and scoop out the flesh, leaving a thick shell.

❦ Heat the oil in a frying pan, and add the garlic and celery. Stir for 1 minute, then add the chicken and cook over medium heat until lightly browned.

❦ Stir in the tomato purée, lime juice and chilli sauce.

❦ Heat until boiling, then stir in the potato flesh, and season with celery salt and pepper.

❦ Spoon the mixture back into the potato shells and cover with foil. Place in a preheated oven at 200°C/400°F/gas mark 6 for 10 minutes or until thoroughly heated through.

Scallops in Oyster Sauce

SERVES 4

4 large scallops, or
10–12 queen scallops
15 g/½ oz butter or margarine
1 shallot, finely chopped
½ tsp Chinese five spice powder
3 tbsp oyster sauce
salt and freshly ground black pepper
4 baked potatoes
lemon twists or wedges, to garnish

CUT the corals from the scallops and reserve. Slice the rest into thin strips.

❦ Melt the butter and quickly fry the shallot for about 1 minute, until lightly coloured. Add the spice powder, and stir in the scallops and corals.

❦ Stir-fry for about 1 minute, then add the oyster sauce and heat thoroughly. Season well with salt and pepper.

❦ Cut a slice from the top of each potato and scoop out the flesh, leaving a thick shell. Chop the flesh and mix into the scallops then spoon back into the shells. Serve hot with twists or wedges of lemon.

Shrimp and Spring Onion

SERVES 4

100g/4 oz peeled cooked shrimps
4 spring onions, finely chopped
½ tsp grated lemon zest
½ tsp finely chopped fresh parsley
large pinch of cayenne pepper
50 g/2 oz butter
4 baked potatoes
salt and freshly ground black pepper
extra shrimps and spring onion curls, to garnish

PLACE the shrimps, spring onions, lemon zest, parsley, cayenne and butter in a mixing bowl.

❦ Halve the potatoes and scoop out the flesh into the mixing bowl. Beat together until thoroughly mixed, and season to taste with salt and pepper.

❦ Return the mixture to the potato skins and bake in a preheated oven at 190°C/375°F/gas mark 5 for 5 minutes or until heated through. Serve immediately, garnished with extra shrimps and spring onions curls.

Tuna Niçoise

SERVES 4

2 large baked potatoes
200 g/7 oz can tuna, drained
1 small red onion, chopped
6 pitted black olives, sliced
salt and freshly ground black pepper
50 g/2 oz can anchovy fillets, drained
2 tbsp freshly grated Parmesan cheese

CUT the potatoes in half and scoop out the flesh. Chop roughly and mix with the tuna, onion and olives. Season to taste with salt and pepper.

❦ Spoon back into the potato shells, and arrange the anchovy fillets on top in a lattice pattern.

❦ Sprinkle with the Parmesan cheese, and place in a preheated oven at 200°C/400°F/gas mark 6 for 10 minutes or until golden brown. Serve hot.

Sardine, Dill and Cucumber

SERVES 4

4 baked potatoes
175 g/6 oz can sardines in tomato sauce
1 tbsp chopped fresh dill
5 cm/2 inch piece cucumber, diced
salt and freshly ground black pepper
parsley sprigs, to garnish

CUT a deep cross in the potatoes and press the sides to open out slightly. Scoop out the flesh.

❦ Discard any bones from the sardines and mash with a fork, then mix into the potato flesh.

❦ Stir in the dill and cucumber, and season generously with salt and pepper.

❦ Spoon the sardine mixture into the potatoes and serve garnished with parsley sprigs.

Smoked Salmon and Asparagus

SERVES 4

4 baked potatoes
4 tbsp crème fraîche
or fromage frais
50 g/2 oz smoked salmon
100 g/4 oz cooked or canned
asparagus tips, drained
and chopped
finely grated zest of ½ lemon
freshly ground black pepper

CUT a slice from the top of each potato and carefully scoop out the flesh with a teaspoon, leaving a thick shell.

❦ Mash the potato with the crème fraîche. Slice the salmon into thin strips, roughly chop half the asparagus, and stir into the mashed potato with the lemon zest.

❦ Season to taste with salt and pepper. Spoon the mixture back into the shells and top each with the reserved asparagus tips.

Salmon and Soured Cream

SERVES 4

225 g/8 oz cold poached salmon
(or drained can)
300 ml/½ pint soured cream
1 tsp lemon juice
salt and freshly ground black pepper
2 tsp chopped fresh or
½ tsp dried thyme
4 baked potatoes
50 g/2 oz flaked almonds, toasted,
to garnish

REMOVE the skin from the salmon. Flake the flesh, removing any bones, and place in a mixing bowl.

❦ Carefully stir in the remaining filling ingredients, taking care not to break up the salmon flesh too much.

❦ Cut a cross in the top of each baked potato, and squeeze gently to open them up. Spoon over the filling, and garnish with the almonds.

Creamy Prawn

SERVES 4

150 ml/¼ pint mayonnaise
1 tbsp tomato purée
1 tbsp chopped fresh parsley
175 g/6 oz peeled cooked prawns
few drops of Tabasco sauce
4 baked potatoes

PLACE the mayonnaise, tomato purée and parsley in a mixing bowl, and mix well together. Stir in the prawns, and season to taste with 2-3 drops of Tabasco.
❦ Cut a cross in the top of each baked potato and squeeze gently to open them up. Spoon over the prawn topping, and serve immediately.

VARIATION: peel and dice the flesh of a ripe avocado, and stir into the mixture with the prawns.

Mussels and Emmenthal

SERVES 4

4 baked potatoes
100 g/4 oz cooked or canned mussels, without shells
2 tbsp chopped fresh parsley
2 tbsp chopped fresh coriander
salt and freshly ground black pepper
50 g/2 oz Emmenthal cheese, grated
2 tbsp wholemeal breadcrumbs
1 garlic clove, crushed

CUT a slice from the top of each potato and scoop out the flesh, leaving a thick shell.
❦ Mix the potato flesh, mussels and half the herbs together and season well with salt and pepper. Spoon back into the shells.
❦ Mix together the remaining herbs, cheese, breadcrumbs and garlic. Spoon over the potatoes.
❦ Place on a baking sheet and bake in a preheated oven at 200°C/400°F/gas mark 6 for 10 minutes, or until golden brown and bubbling. Serve hot.

Tuna and Onion

SERVES 4

200 g/7 oz can tuna, drained
6 tbsp mayonnaise
6 spring onions, trimmed and chopped
grated zest of 1 lemon
4 baked potatoes
salt and freshly ground black pepper

PLACE the tuna, mayonnaise, spring onions and grated lemon zest in a mixing bowl.

❦ Halve the potatoes and scoop out the flesh into the mixing bowl. Beat well together until thoroughly mixed, and season to taste with salt and pepper.

❦ Pile the filling back into the potato shells, and brown them under a preheated grill. Serve immediately.

Cod Creole Wedges

SERVES 4

225 g/8 oz cod fillet, skinned
2 tsp lime or lemon juice
1 small onion, finely chopped
1 celery stick, chopped
1 small green pepper, seeded and sliced
2 tsp olive oil
¼ tsp cayenne pepper
¼ tsp garlic salt
2 medium tomatoes, skinned and chopped
4 potatoes, baked as wedges (see page 5)

CUT the cod into bite-sized chunks. Sprinkle with the lime or lemon juice.

❦ In a large pan, heat the olive oil and fry the onion, celery and pepper over low heat until softened. Add the cayenne pepper and garlic salt.

❦ Stir in the cod with the chopped tomatoes. Bring to the boil, then cover and simmer for about 5 minutes or until the fish flakes easily.

❦ Divide the potato wedges between 4 plates and spoon the fish into the centre. Serve hot.

Chilli Prawn Salsa with Potato Skins

SERVES 4

1 garlic clove, skinned
1 fresh green chilli, seeded
1 small yellow pepper, halved and seeded
3 tomatoes, quartered
1 tbsp olive oil
1 tbsp fresh lime juice
100 g/4 oz peeled cooked prawns
salt and freshly ground black pepper
4 baked potatoes
olive oil, for brushing

To make the salsa, place the garlic, chilli, pepper, tomatoes, oil and lime juice in a blender or food processor and process until finely chopped. Alternatively, chop finely by hand.

❦ Stir in the prawns and season with salt and pepper.

❦ Cut the potatoes into quarters lengthways. Scoop out most of the flesh (use this for another recipe).

❦ Brush the skins with oil and place under a preheated grill for about 5 minutes, turning occasionally, until crisp and golden.

❦ Serve the potato skins hot, with the salsa for dipping.

Thai Fish with Lime and Coriander

SERVES 4

1 tsp grated fresh ginger root
finely grated zest and juice of ½ lime
1 garlic clove, crushed
1 tbsp chopped fresh coriander
1 spring onion, chopped
200 g/7 oz firm white fish fillet, e.g. monkfish, skinned
1 tbsp groundnut or sunflower oil
salt and freshly ground black pepper
4 baked potatoes
lime slices, to garnish

Mix together the ginger, lime, garlic, coriander and onion. Cut the fish into thin strips and toss in the mixture.

❦ Heat the oil and quickly stir-fry the fish mixture until just cooked, taking care not to break it up. Remove from the heat and season to taste with salt and pepper.

❦ Cut a slice from the top of each potato and scoop out the flesh, leaving a thick shell. Stir into the fish mixture, then spoon back into the shells and serve immediately, topped with a slice of lime.

Smoked Mackerel Parsley Fluffs

SERVES 4

15 g/½ oz butter or margarine
15 g/½ oz plain flour
150 ml/¼ pint milk
salt and freshly ground black pepper
2 large baked potatoes
1 egg (size 2), separated
150 g/5 oz smoked mackerel fillets, skinned and chopped
3 tbsp chopped fresh parsley

MELT the butter in a saucepan and stir in the flour. Stir over a moderate heat for about 2 minutes, then gradually stir in the milk.

❦ Cook, stirring, until thickened and smooth. Remove from the heat and season with salt and pepper.

❦ Cut a slice from the top of each potato and scoop out the flesh. Mash until smooth, then beat in the sauce and egg yolks. Fold in the chopped fish and parsley. Season to taste with salt and pepper.

❦ Whisk the egg white until stiff and fold into the potato mixture. Pile back into the shells and place on a baking sheet.

❦ Bake in a preheated oven at 200°C/400°F/gas mark 6 for 18–20 minutes or until well risen and golden brown. Serve immediately.

Smoked Haddock and Dill

SERVES 4

350 g/12 oz smoked haddock
150 ml/¼ pint skimmed milk
150 ml/¼ pint soured cream
2 tbsp chopped fresh dill or chives
salt and freshly ground black pepper
4 baked potatoes

PLACE the fish in a saucepan, and pour over the milk. Cover and cook for about 15 minutes until the flesh flakes easily with a fork.

❦ Drain the fish, discarding the milk. Remove the skin and flake the flesh. Return the fish to the pan, and mix in the soured cream and dill or chives. Season to taste.

❦ Set the pan over a low heat and gently warm the fish through without boiling the mixture.

❦ Cut a cross in the top of each baked potato, and squeeze gently to open them up. Spoon over the fish topping. Serve immediately with a mixed salad.